EASY TO CROSS STITCH

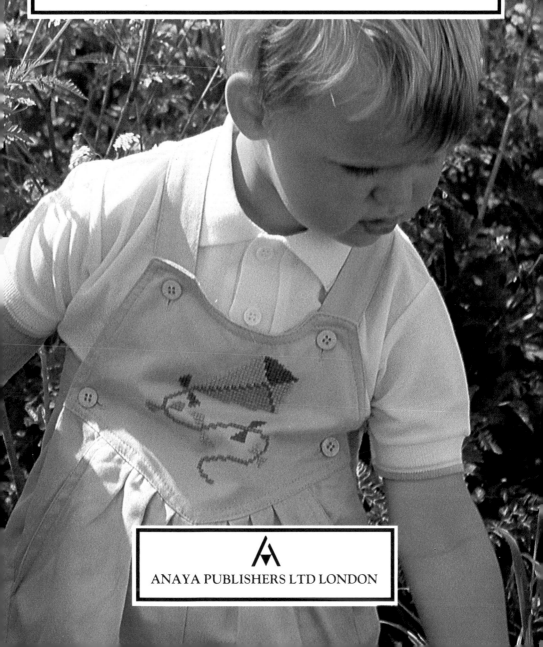

EASY TO CROSS STITCH

Gail Lawther

Series Consultant: Eve Harlow

ANAYA PUBLISHERS LTD LONDON

First published in Great Britain in 1990
by Anaya Publishers Ltd, 49 Neal Street, London WC2H 9PJ

Editor Eve Harlow
Designer Mike Leaman
Photographer Di Lewis
Illustrator Kate Simunek
Charts Julie Ward

British Library Cataloguing in Publication Data

Lawther, Gail
Easy to cross stitch.—(Easy to make)
1. Embroidery.   Cross-stitch
I. Title   II. Series
746.443
ISBN 1-85470-081-2

Typeset by Tradespools Limited, Frome, Somerset

Colour Reproduction by Columbia Offset, Singapore

Printed and bound in Great Britain by Clays Ltd., Bungay, Suffolk

CONTENTS

Introduction

The revival of cross stitch combines an ancient embroidery technique with modern fabrics and threads, producing items that are practical enough for everyday use but pretty enough to become heirlooms.

Cross stitch is found in embroidery traditions throughout the world, in the Middle East, in eastern Europe, the Balkans, South America and, of course, in Europe. Patterns have been handed down for generations from mother to daughter, and in the middle east in particular, some cross stitch designs have been used for women's robes for more than 2000 years.

Cross stitch was used for children's samplers in Victorian England and many of these samplers still survive, some of them worked by girls as young as 5 or 6 years old. While many crafts have been revived in recent years, cross stitch was left behind for a while – perhaps those samplers made it seem like hard work! But, happily, cross stitch has now come back into favour, and been updated to suit a modern generation. Beautiful fabrics and sumptuous threads lend themselves wonderfully to cross stitch designs, and through this book you'll see just how versatile this needlecraft can be.

Worldwide inspiration

In keeping with the international nature of cross stitch, you'll find designs inspired by many different traditions, from Oriental fans to Amerindian blankets. There is even a bookmark based on Egyptian hieroglyphics. The fabrics used are as varied as possible, from conventional hardanger to hessian and even paper! The threads that can be used for cross stitch are even more varied – pearl cotton, soft cotton, wool, metallic threads, stranded cottons, and beautiful, shiny, synthetic threads. Throughout this book, the patterns and techniques are kept as simple as possible, so that even beginners can produce professional-looking results.

Fabrics

Cross stitch is one of the counted thread embroidery techniques and therefore fabrics with an even weave are mostly used. Evenweave fabrics incude woven cotton or cotton mixes, linen, hessian and some specially woven embroidery fabrics.

Charts

Counted thread embroidery designs are mostly worked from charts with colours or symbols indicating where cross stitches should be placed. Colour charts are used in this book, and these are very easy to follow. Always check the instructions before starting a project to see how many strands of thread are used and how many threads of the background fabric are covered with cross stitches. To work from a chart, you should first find and mark the middle of your fabric with basting threads or with a chalk pencil. The middle of the chart is indicated by arrows on the edges. Start your embroidery in the middle of the design and work outwards.

Here the first stage of the stitch is worked from right to
left. To complete the cross work from left to right

Working cross stitch
Cross stitch may be worked from right to left
or left to right (see illustration) but the
upper stitch of the cross must always lie in
the same direction throughout a piece of
work.

Equipment
You need very little equipment for working
the designs in this book. An embroidery
hoop or frame is useful but not essential,
because small pieces of embroidery can be
worked in the hand. You will need different
types of embroidery needles (depending on
the thread being used), sharp embroidery
scissors, some coloured basting thread or a
dressmaker's chalk pencil and the usual
contents of a sewing basket.

1: HOUSE
AND HOME

Going Greek

The ancient Greek key pattern, sometimes called the Meander Pattern, is used for these smart napkin rings. They could be worked to tone with the table mats on page 14, or embroider the rings in different colour schemes for each member of the family.

Materials (for six rings)
Six pieces of cream Aida cloth 8 × 3in (20 × 7.5cm), 11 threads to 1in (2.5cm)
Anchor stranded cottons as follows: five skeins of 295 pale yellow, six skeins of 303 dark yellow, two skeins of 316 pale orange, two skeins of 335 dark orange
Cardboard tube 1½in (37mm) diameter (or stiff card and sticky tape; see this page)
Clear adhesive
Yellow fabric (or paper) for lining.

Preparation
1 Measure and mark the middle of the fabric both vertically and horizontally with basting stitches.

Working the embroidery
2 The centre of the chart for the Greek key pattern is indicated by arrows at the edges and these coincide with your basted stitches. Following the chart and the key, begin embroidery in the middle of the design, using 4 strands of thread together. Work the area shown on the chart.

Finishing
3 Press the finished embroidery on the wrong side lightly. Measure to check that the embroidery is square. If it has distorted in working, lightly spray the wrong side of the embroidery with water, gently pull into shape, pin down at corners and leave to dry. Trim excess fabric back to within ½in (1cm) of the embroidery.

Making the napkin rings
4 Using a sharp crafts knife, cut rings from the cardboard tube, 1½in (37mm) thick.

5 Spread glue thinly on the back of the embroidery. Smooth the fabric onto the cardboard ring, overlapping the short ends and glueing down. Fold and glue the long edges of the fabric to the inside of the ring.

6 Cut strips of yellow fabric (or paper) to line the ring. Spread glue thinly on the back and press to the inside of the ring. Leave to dry. Make five more rings in the same way.

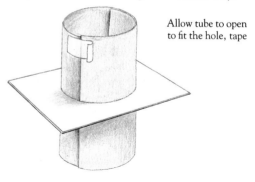

Allow tube to open to fit the hole, tape

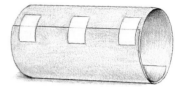

Tape the tube, cut as required

Making cardboard rings
Using a pair of compasses, draw a 1½in (37mm) diameter circle on thin, stiff card. Cut another piece of card 4¹/₂in (11cm) long by 1½in (37mm). Roll up, insert in the hole, allow to open. Tape the join and remove. Cut rings as required.

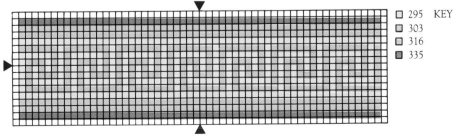

KEY
□ 295
□ 303
□ 316
■ 335

Turkish delight

Go for the classical look with these table napkins, embroidered with a traditional motif taken from Turkish rugs. To complete the classical effect, team them with the Greek key napkin rings (page 10) and the Roman mosaic table mats (page 14), using toning colours – or work them in a different scheme to match your dinner service.

KEY
■ 46
■ 351
■ Bronze metallic

Materials
Six linen napkins
Anchor stranded cottons as follows: one skein of 351 brown, two skeins of 46 red
Bronze metallic thread.

Preparation
1 First, check the weave of the napkin in both directions. Some linen fabrics have more threads in one direction than the other; lay a ruler horizontally over the threads and count how many there are to an inch (or centimetre), then lay the ruler the other way and count how many threads there are in the other direction.

2 If the napkins have more threads in one direction than the other, work with the tightly-spaced threads running horizontally; this will mean that the design will come out square, as in the picture. If your napkins have the same number of threads to the inch (or centimetre) in both directions, the design will come out rectangular, as in the chart.

Working the embroidery
3 Using three strands of red thread together, begin working the design 1½in (37mm) in from the right and bottom edges of the napkin.

4 Using three strands of metallic thread together, work the bronze border inside the red border. Complete the motif, using three strands of red and three strands of brown thread.

5 Embroider the remaining five napkins in the same way. (If you prefer to make your own napkins, use a coloured, evenweave embroidery linen and finish the edges as for the mats on page 14).

Finishing
6 Use a cool iron to press the embroidery on the wrong side. Place a piece of tissue paper between embroidery and iron. Take care not to use an iron that is too hot or the metallic threads may melt.

If you find it difficult to buy the metallic thread, substitute Anchor shade 339 instead; you will need one skein.

Modern mosaic

Shaded Roman mosaic patterns provided the inspiration for this simple repeat design; work it on a set of table mats and, if you're feeling inspired, you could repeat it round the hem of a matching tablecloth.

Materials (for six mats)
Six pieces of orange hessian 21 × 15in
  (53 × 38cm), 16 threads to 1in (2.5cm)
Orange sewing thread
Anchor tapisserie wools as follows: two
  skeins each of 332 pale orange, 333
  mid-orange, 334 dark orange, 748 light
  red, 13 rich red.

Preparation
1 Work a line of narrow machine zigzag stitches 1½in (37mm) from the edges on the pieces of hessian.

Working the embroidery
2 Following the chart and starting at A, begin working the pattern over two threads of the fabric, 1½in (37mm) up from the bottom edge of the fabric and 2in (5cm) in from the left-hand edge.

3 Fit in as many complete repeats of the pattern (A–B) as you can, to within 1½in (37mm) of the top edge (19 or 20 repeats).

4 Work the embroidery on the remaining mats in the same way.

5 Press the embroidered mats on the wrong side using a warm iron, making sure that vertical and horizontal threads are running square.

Finishing
6 Fringe the mats by snipping into the fabric edges, at 1in (2.5cm) intervals, almost up to the stitching line. Pull out threads. For a different finish turn under a single hem and stitch with wide zigzag of machine-stitching, using matching or contrasting thread. Alternatively, bind the edges with orange bias binding.

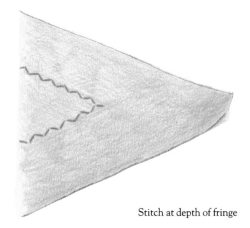

Stitch at depth of fringe

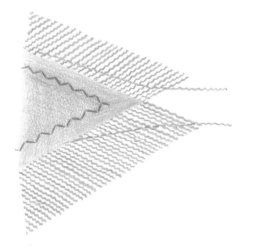

Pull out threads

The mosaic pattern is also suitable for working matching napkin rings. The depth of the pattern can be extended as you desire. You might use some bronze-coloured metallic thread to oversew the edges.

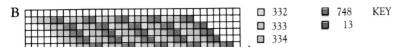

B

			332		748	KEY
			333		13	
			334			

A

Shades of lavender

If the idea of embroidering an entire tablecloth seems a little daunting, cheat a little by painting designs with fabric paints then embellish with cross stitches to give texture to the design.

Materials

Circular tablecloth approximately 70in (175cm) diameter

Squared dressmaker's pattern paper, one square = 1in (2.5cm)

Dressmaker's carbon paper

Fabric paints or fabric painting crayons in green, purple, white

Paintbrushes of different sizes

Anchor stranded cottons as follows: one skein each of purple 112, 109, 99, 96 and 95.

Preparation

1 Trace the lavender sprays on page 18. Fold the tablecloth in half, then quarters. Using dressmaker's carbon paper, transfer the lavender sprays to the cloth, stems 1½in (37mm) from the hem and heads towards the centre. Space them as desired. Unfold the cloth and transfer the design to the second quarter. Complete the rest of the tablecloth, so that there are lavender sprays all round. (If you prefer, you can draw the lavender sprays directly on to the cloth.)

2 Spread the tablecloth on several layers of clean newspaper on a flat surface. Mix the green paint, brush in the stems and leaves, working one quarter of the cloth at a time. Leave to dry before working the next quarter. Next, paint in the lavender heads using the brush almost dry and with free strokes.

3 When painting is completed and the paint quite dry, fix the paint following the manufacturer's instructions.

Working the embroidery

4 Using six strands of thread together, work random cross stitches over the lavender heads, using all five shades, keeping the darker colours near to the bottom of the heads and the lighter near the top.

5 If you wish, you could also work a few straight stitches on the leaves using six closely related green tones, such as the range in Anchor colours 262 and 260.

The fabric painting technique can be used on other projects in this book. For instance, try painting some of the motifs for the sampler on page 47, adding a few cross stitches afterwards for texture and additional colour.

Trace these two
sprays of lavender
and transfer to the
table cloth, or copy
them and draw them in
place using an
embroidery pencil

18

Work cross
stitches on
the painted
lavender heads
using purple shades,
dark tones at
the bottom and
paler tones near the top.

Set lavender sprays
all round the edges
of the tablecloth with
heads towards the centre.

19

Scandinavian tulips

Embroider a table runner to display your ornaments, or to make a dressing table even prettier. Tulips often feature in painted and embroidered designs from Norway, Sweden and Denmark; this one is worked in subtle shades of pink and grey-green, but you could also use a different bright colour for each pair of tulips, yellow, red and blue or turquoise to make the design even more eye-catching.

Materials

Piece of white evenweave fabric 24 × 14in (60 × 35cm), 28–30 threads to 1in (2.5cm)

Anchor stranded cottons as follows: two skeins each of 40 pink, 876 green.

Preparation

1 Work a line of narrow machine-zigzag stitches 1in (2.5cm) from the edge all round (see page 14).

Working the embroidery

2 Following the chart and starting at A, begin the embroidery 3in (7.5cm) up from the long edge and from the left-hand edge. Use four strands of thread together throughout and work stitches over four threads of fabric.

3 Repeat the design along the other long edge, making sure that the stems are still on the outside edge of the runner with the flowers towards the centre.

Finishing

4 When the embroidery is completed, press on the wrong side with a warm iron. Fringe the edges as described for the table mats on page 14.

> This motif is ideal for working on cross stitch border tape. Stitch the tape to fabric for a shelf edging

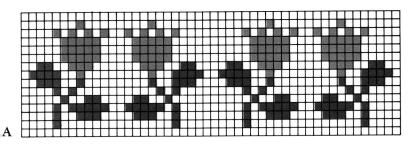

A

■ 40
■ 376

21

Traditional prettiness

Welcome guests by putting out a hand-embroidered fingertip towel for their use. This one is decorated with a delicate design of pinks and forget-me-not flowers which you can work to the colour scheme given, or choose one of your own.

Materials
White fingertip towel with border 32 threads wide
Anchor pearl cotton as follows: one skein each of 54 dark pink, 52 light pink, 203 green, 290 yellow, 131 blue.

Note: If a suitable towel cannot be purchased, work the design on white evenweave embroidery fabric, turn under the edges about ¼ in (6mm) all round and sew or machine-stitch the strip to the towel when the embroidery is completed. This type of decoration is ideal for making a set of towels for a new bride, or for a girl setting up in her own home.

Working the embroidery
Following the chart and key begin working the design on the left-hand bottom edge of the border. Work each cross stitch over two fabric threads. Repeat the section of the design as indicated on the chart.

Cross-stitch tape (see page 34) could also be used for a towel, or the waste canvas method described on page 36 could be used. This border design has other uses in embroidery of household linens. It would look pretty on a white hessian tablecloth with matching napkins, or on a set of table mats. Or you might work the border on pillowcases, using white cotton on white, or matching a pastel colour to the fabric on coloured linens.

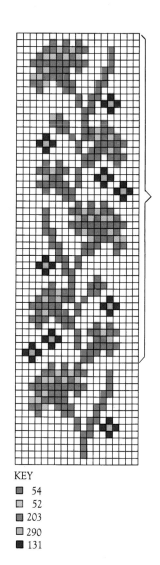

KEY
■ 54
□ 52
■ 203
□ 290
■ 131

Bold and bright

African beadwork designs have been translated here into two colourful cushion covers that will brighten up your living room.

Materials (for two cushions)
2 pieces of Binca fabric 15in (38cm) square,
    6 threads to 1in (2.5cm)
4 pieces of backing fabric 15 × 10in
    (38 × 25.5cm)
Double knitting yarn as follows: 1 ball each
    of purple, dark blue, light blue, green,
    red, aqua and yellow.

Note: Double knitting wools vary slightly in
thickness, so experiment first to make sure
that the stitches cover the fabric. On a waste
piece of Binca, work two or three cross
stitches using four strands of wool across two
holes. If the wool covers the background
so that no canvas can be seen behind,
work the designs with four strands of wool
throughout. If the work looks a little
'gappy', use five strands.

Working the embroidery
1 Work the designs on the Binca over two
holes, following the charts and starting at A.

2 When the embroidery is completed, press
the work lightly on the wrong side with a
warm iron, pulling gently into shape so that
the fabric is square.

Making the cushion
3 Turn under, press and machine-stitch one
long edge on each piece of backing fabric.

4 Trim the embroidered pieces back to
within ¾in (2cm) of the stitches.

5 Pin and baste the backing pieces together,
overlapping the neatened edges, so that the
back is the same size as the embroidery.

6 Machine-stitch all round, stitching on
the edge of the embroidery. Stitch over the
same line again for extra strength.

7 Trim the seams to within ½in (12mm) of
the stitching, and clip the corners. Turn
right side out and press.

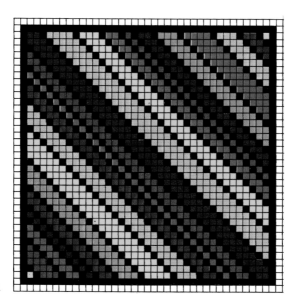

A

Colours on the charts are those listed in
materials – purple, dark blue, light blue,
black, green, red, aqua and yellow

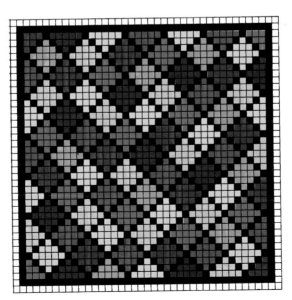

A

25

2: BABIES AND CHILDREN

Bright comforter

Cotton gingham is ideal for making cot quilts because it washes so easily and you can use the pattern for placing cross stitches in decorative patterns. Work the embroidery through the fabric, wadding and muslin backing to achieve a quilted effect.

Materials
Piece of gingham with ¼in (6mm) checks, 44 × 28in (112 × 72cm) wide
Piece of medium-weight washable polyester wadding the same size
Piece of muslin the same size
Piece of matching, plain fabric for backing the quilt, 50 × 33in (128 × 84cm)
Anchor stranded cottons as follows: two skeins each of 88 red, 110 mauve.

Preparation
1 Baste the gingham, wadding and muslin together round the edges and then across vertically and horizontally, thus marking the middle.

Working the embroidery
2 The middle of the chart 1 is indicated by arrows which correspond with the middle of the fabric marked with basting. Using three strands of mauve and three strands of red, work the design in double cross stitch (see diagram), starting in the middle, and working on white squares.

3 Work chart 2 design, using three strands of red thread, 13 check squares in from the edges at each corner, working double cross stitches on white squares.

Finishing
4 Remove the horizontal and vertical basting threads. Pin and baste the quilt right side up on the plain backing fabric, wrong sides together.

5 Turn the backing fabric edges onto the quilt with a narrow hem and work hemming stitches all round or, if you prefer, machine-stitch the hem. Fold the corners neatly. Remove any basting threads that still show.

Chart 1   Chart 2

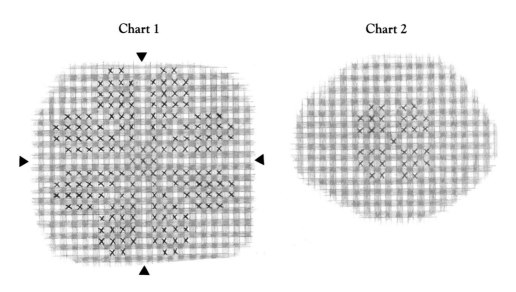

Welcome to the world

Combine a greeting and a delightful gift with one of these made-to-keep birth congratulation cards. The cards may be framed afterwards for nursery pictures. Adapt the ABC card to carry the baby's initials, and the date of birth, worked from the alphabet chart overleaf.

Materials
Teddy bear
Piece of white Aida fabric 4 × 5in (10 × 12.5cm), 14 threads to 1 in (2.5cm)

Anchor stranded cottons as follows: one skein each of 403 black, 334 red, 361 pale beige, 890 beige, 208 green, 359 brown

Cream oval-window card blank.

ABC card
Piece of white Aida fabric 4 × 5in (10 × 12.5cm), 14 threads to 1in (2.5cm)

Anchor stranded cottons as follows; one skein each of 128 blue, 24 pink, 301 yellow, 204 green

White round-window card blank.

Bootee card
Piece of white Aida fabric 4 × 5in) (10 × 12.5cm), 11 threads to 1in (2.5cm)

Anchor stranded cottons as follows: one skein each of 144 blue (or 24 pink), 01 white

12in (30cm) piece of white satin ribbon ¹/₄in (6mm)-wide

Blue round-window card blank.

Preparation
1 Measure and mark the middle of the fabric with lines of basting stitches, vertically and horizontally.

Working and embroidery
2 The middle of charts is indicated by arrows on the edges. This corresponds with the middle of your fabric, marked with basting.

Teddy bear
3 Work the design from chart 1 following the key and starting in the middle. Use three strands of thread together. Work the balloon string in back stitch using one strand of black thread.

ABC card
4 Work the design from chart 2, following the key and using four strands of thread together for cross stitches. If initials are required, work from selected letters in chart 4. Use three strands of green thread to work the child's date of birth, if desired, following chart 4.

Bootee card
5 Work the design from chart 3, following the key and using four strands of thread together for cross stitches. Use one strand of thread for back stitches where marked on the chart. Work a single diagonal stitch or half a cross stitch where indicated on the chart.

Finishing
6 Cut the ribbon in half and thread one piece through from the back of the embroidery so that the ends emerge at each side of one bootee. Tie in a neat bow. Repeat with the second piece of ribbon on the second bootee.

Mounting the embroidery
7 Trim the fabric so that it fits behind the window of the card. Spread glue thinly around the inside of the window, place the embroidery in position and press down firmly. Spread glue on the back of the third fold, fold and press down onto the back of the embroidery.

31

Chart 4

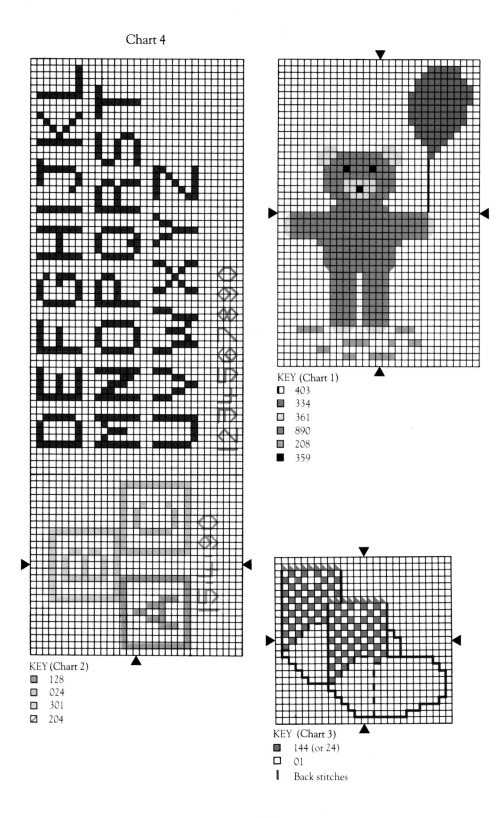

KEY (Chart 1)
- 403
- 334
- 361
- 890
- 208
- 359

KEY (Chart 2)
- 128
- 024
- 301
- 204

KEY (Chart 3)
- 144 (or 24)
- 01
- Back stitches

Spread glue round window
and on the third fold

Place embroidery in position
press down firmly

Sun flowers

A simple sundress can be made into something special by adding borders of cross stitch flowers to the hem and waist. A matching hairband would make an outfit pretty enough for a party.

Materials
Sundress to fit ages 3–4
White cross stitch border tape with blue edging, 14 threads to 1in (2.5cm)
Anchor stranded cottons as follows: 8 skeins of 145 blue, 1 skein of 57 dark pink, 4 skeins of 40 light pink
Small piece of ¼in (6mm)-wide elastic for hairband.

Note: To estimate tape quantities measure round the dress at the waist and hem, add 2in (5cm) for seam allowance on each piece. Allow 14in (36cm) for a hairband.

Preparation
1 Measure and mark the centre of each piece of tape.

Working the embroidery
2 Following the chart and key (the centre of the design is indicated by arrows), begin embroidery in the centre of the tape and work towards the ends. Use six strands of thread together, and work each stitch across two threads of fabric.

Finishing
3 Turn under the short ends of the embroidered tapes for the sundress, and appliqué them in position on the dress by hand (using hemming) or machine-stitching.

Alternatively, a better finish is achieved by opening the dress side-seams where the tape is to be applied. Apply the tape flat to front and back, then re-stitch the seams.

Hairband
4 Turn and sew the short edges of the hairband to neaten, cut and pin on a piece of elastic so that the hairband will fit the child's head. Sew the elastic into place.

Stitch the embroidered tape to the skirt pieces

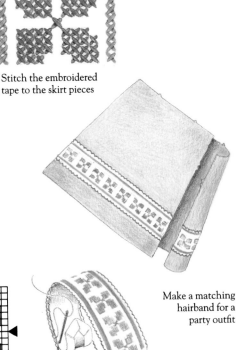

Make a matching hairband for a party outfit

KEY ■ 145
　　 ▨ 57
　　 ☐ 40

Flying high

Cross stitch doesn't always have to be done on canvas or on evenweave fabric; use the waste canvas method to embroider pretty designs – such as this kite – on ready-made children's clothes.

Materials
Pair of child's dungarees with a plain bib
measuring at least 4in (10cm) square
Anchor stranded cottons as follows: one
skein each of 110 mauve, 433 blue, 227
green, 86 pink, 298 yellow, 119 purple
Piece of waste canvas, 5in (12.5cm) square,
11 threads to 1in (2.5cm).

Preparation
1 Baste the waste canvas to the dungarees
over the area where the motif is to be
worked. Mark the middle with horizontal
and vertical lines of basting stitches.

Working the embroidery
2 The middle of the design on the chart is
indicated by arrows. This corresponds with
the middle of your fabric, marked with
basting threads.

3 Using four strands of thread together,
embroider the design through the canvas
and the fabric, following the chart and the
key and starting in the middle.

Finishing
4 When the embroidery is completed,
remove the basting threads and dampen the
canvas; this dissolves the glue holding the
canvas together.

5 Pull the vertical and horizontal strands of
the canvas out from under the cross stitches,
until only the embroidery remains on the
dungarees.

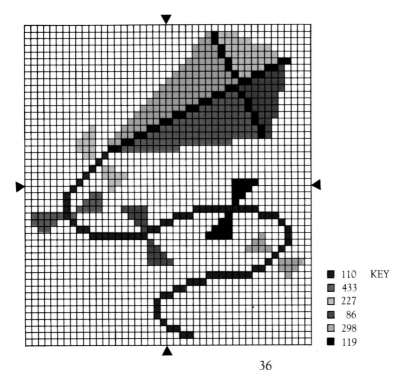

	KEY
■ 110	
■ 433	
□ 227	
■ 86	
□ 298	
■ 119	

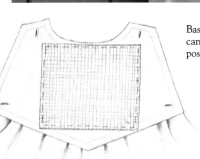

Baste the waste
canvas in
position

Embroider the
design on the canvas

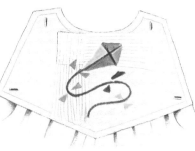

Dampen, then
withdraw the canvas
threads

3D dazzler

Babies love watching bright colours; dangle this cross-stitch mobile over a cot to provide visual stimulation. It's worked on cross-stitch paper, so it isn't robust enough to play with; hang it out of reach but where the bright colours will catch the light.

Materials

Sheets of cross stitch paper in white, red, green and gold

Anchor stranded cottons as follows: one skein each of 433 blue, 298 yellow, 119 purple, 86 pink

Transparent plastic thread (for stringing the mobile)

Crafts knife

White card

Coloured papers in blue, red, green and pink

Clear glue.

Preparation

1 Cut squares from the cross stitch paper to the following sizes (dimensions are for complete holes so, if the square is 81 holes along each edge, cut the paper on the 82nd hole):

White – 1 square 81 × 81 holes
Red – 1 square 61 × 61 holes
Green – 1 square 41 × 41 holes
Gold – 1 square 21 × 21 holes.

2 Use the crafts knife to cut out the centre of each square, leaving a frame of five complete holes wide.

Working the embroidery

3 Using six strands of thread together and following the chart on pages 40–41 for colours, work cross stitches over two holes round the frames. (Note that the chart is in two pieces and is joined where indicated with arrows.)

Finishing

4 Brush glue sparingly on to the back of each embroidered frame and stick onto the white card. Press down firmly.

5 When the glue is dry, cut out the four mounted, embroidered frames.

6 Glue each frame to coloured paper, cut out when dry.

7 Thread a sharp, strong needle with the transparent thread and string the mobile sections together, the largest at the top.

Cut the centre from the squares

Glue squares to card, then cut out

Cut frames out when dry

38

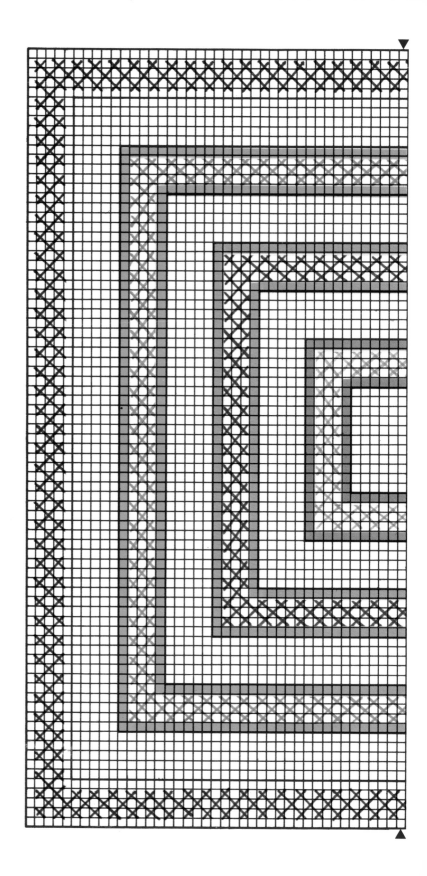

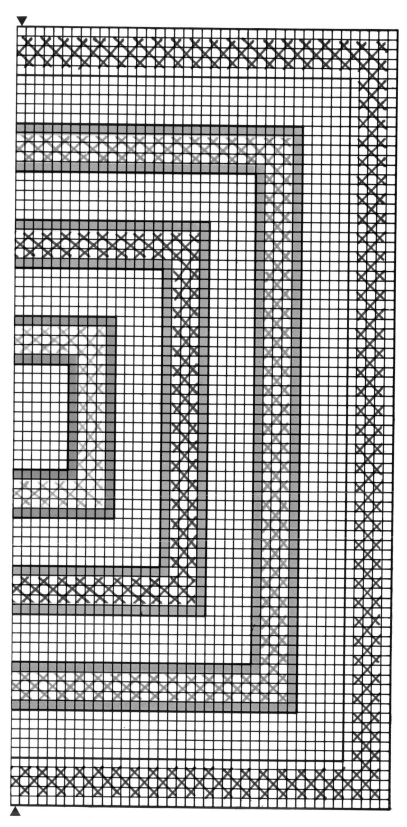

Chart for
3-D dazzler

Join chart
sections where
indicated with
arrows. Follow
the colours on
the chart for
embroidery

Colonial charmer

Samplers are always favourite cross-stitch designs, and this one is based on some of the many American Colonial patterns. Stitch one for a special friend or a young child, or indulge yourself with one to decorate your own home.

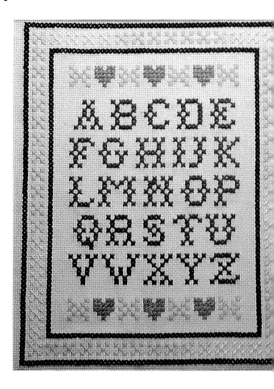

Materials
Piece of pale green Aida cloth, 14 × 18in (35 × 45cm), 14 threads to 1in (2.5cm)
Anchor stranded cottons as follows: one skein each of 204 pale green, 290 dark yellow; two skeins each of 1217 variegated yellow, 923 dark green, 230 mid-green
Piece of Pres-On adhesive board to fit your chosen picture frame
Masking tape.

Preparation
1 Measure and mark the middle of the fabric with lines of basting stitches, vertically and horizontally.

Working the embroidery
2 The middle of the sampler chart is indicated by arrows on the edges. This corresponds with the middle of your fabric, marked with basting.

3 Using six strands of thread together, and working across two threads of the canvas each way, work the design, following the chart and key. Work the border first, then complete the design, counting threads to position the motifs and letters.

Finishing
4 When the embroidery is completed, press lightly on the wrong side.

Mounting the sampler
5 Peel the protective covering from the Pres-On board, and position the embroidery on top. Smooth the fabric onto the sticky surface, from the centre outwards.

6 Turn the excess fabric onto the back of the board, secure with masking tape. The sampler is now ready for framing.

The finished size of this sampler is approximately 12 x 10in (30 x 25cm) but you could enlarge it on a bigger piece of fabric by working the border sides longer. You might also add one or two of the motifs from page 47. The row of houses could go across the bottom under the hearts and flowers.

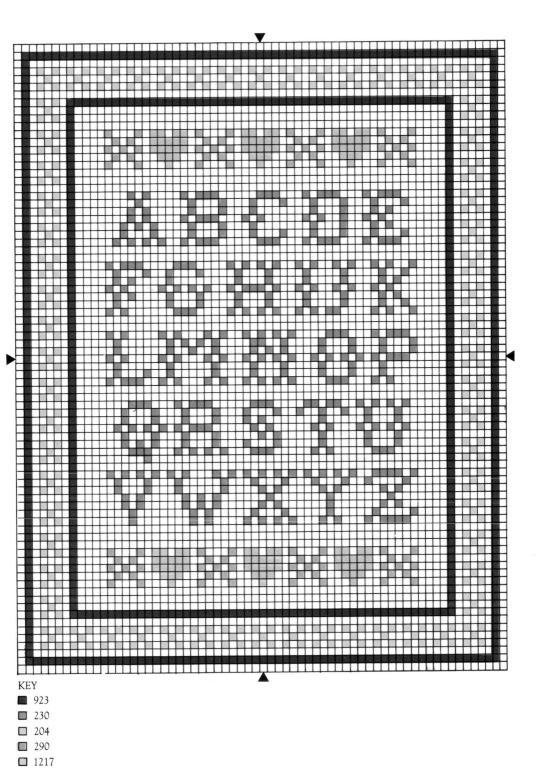

KEY
- ■ 923
- ■ 230
- ☐ 204
- ■ 290
- ☐ 1217

Over to you

Samplers aren't just for new babies; they can be for new homes, new marriages, or for birthdays, anniversaries or any special occasion. Why not design your own? Choose from these borders and motifs, and work out your own design on squared paper.

Designing a sampler

Sampler designs are first worked out on squared paper. Decide the finished size then choose your fabric. (The motifs and borders can be worked to any size you like.) Squares on the squared paper represent cross stitches, worked over a pair of threads, or over three or four threads. It is up to you. It is a good idea to experiment with a few stitches on your chosen fabric first. Once decided, mark the middle of the graph paper with vertical and horizontal lines. Supposing your fabric has a count of 14 threads to 1in (2.5cm) and the sampler is to be 12in (30cm) wide. If you have decided to work cross stitches over two threads, then every square on the paper is two threads. You therefore count off 168 squares across the graph paper for the width of your sampler. Work out the depth in the same way.

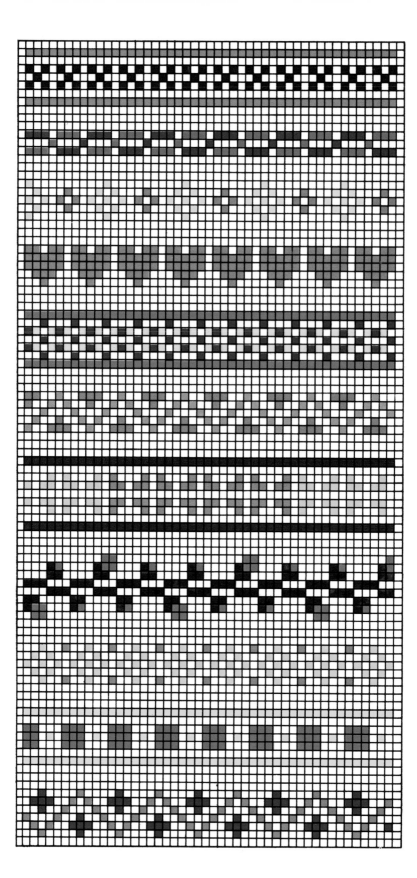

3: THE PERSONAL TOUCH

Indian stripes

The bold diagonal stripes of American Indian blankets inspired this geometrical design; work it small as a pincushion, or use thicker threads on larger mesh canvas for an eye-catching cushion-cover.

Materials

Two pieces of blue Binca fabric, 5in (13cm) square, eight threads to 1in (2.5cm)

Two pieces of lightweight iron-on interfacing, 5in (13cm) square

Anchor stranded cottons as follows: one skein each of 147 dark blue, 131 mid blue, 130 light blue, 306 dark yellow, 305 mid-yellow, 293 light yellow

Gold metallic thread

Small amount of polyester toy filling.

Working the embroidery

1 Starting at A, two threads in from the left-hand and bottom edges of the fabric and using six strands of thread together, work the design following the chart and key. For the gold squares, use four strands of the metallic thread together. Work both pieces of Binca with the design.

Finishing

2 When the embroidery is completed, press on the wrong side lightly with a warm iron.

3 Iron the interfacing onto the wrong sides of the embroidered squares to prevent the edges from fraying and give firmer handling.

4 Place the two squares of Binca together right sides facing. Sew by hand or machine-stitch round three sides, stitching just next to the embroidery.

5 Cut the corners of the fabric off diagonally, turn right side out.

6 Stuff the pincushion with filling. Turn in the raw edges level with the embroidery and pin. Slipstitch the edges together or, if you prefer, use tiny oversewing stitches.

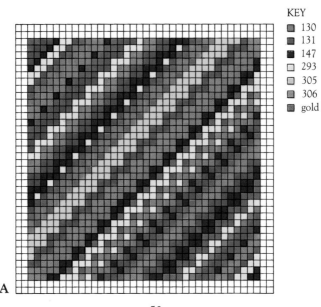

KEY
- 130
- 131
- 147
- 293
- 305
- 306
- gold

A

For quiet times

Curling up with a favourite book is always a pleasure – and even more of a pleasure when you can find your page marked with an Egyptian-design bookmark. Embroider yourself a special case for your spectacles too – this design was inspired by Eskimo leatherwork.

Bookmark
Materials
White Stitch 'n Metal bookmark blank
Anchor stranded cottons as follows: one skein each of 139 blue, 88 pink, 112 purple, 229 green, 46 red, 01 white
Gold metallic thread.

Working the embroidery
Using three strands of thread or three strands of gold thread together, work the bookmark following the chart and the key.

Spectacles case
Materials
Two pieces of cream Binca fabric, 4 × 9in (10 × 23cm), six threads to 1in (2.5cm)
Anchor soft cottons as follows: one skein each of 297 yellow, 47 red, 147 blue, 189 green
Two pieces each of medium-weight iron-on interfacing and lining, same size.

Preparation
1 Measure and mark the middle of both pieces of fabric with lines of basting stitches, vertically and horizontally.

Working the embroidery
2 The middle of the chart is indicated by arrows on the edges. This corresponds with the middle of your fabric, marked with basting.

3 Using the soft cotton, work the design from the chart and key on both pieces of Binca fabric. Finish thread off neatly at the back so that it cannot be seen from the front of the work.

Finishing
4 Iron the interfacing onto the back of the finished embroidery to prevent fraying.

5 Trim the fabric back to within four holes of the embroidery at the top, and to within two holes on the other three edges.

6 Fold the top edges under and sew down by hand or machine-stitch.

7 Place the two pieces of embroidery together right sides facing, sew or machine-stitch round three sides, leaving the top open. Clip the corners diagonally, turn right side out.

8 Stitch the lining pieces together on three sides, right sides facing. Trim seam allowances back to $\frac{1}{4}$in (6mm), slip into the case, slipstitch to case on the open end.

KEY to spectacles case
- 297
- 47
- 147
- 189

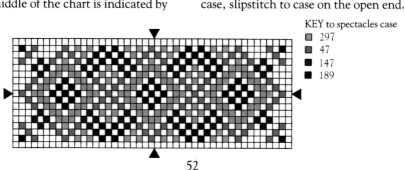

52

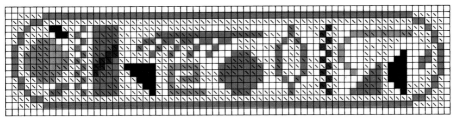

KEY to bookmark
- ■ 139
- ■ 88
- ■ 112
- ■ 229
- ■ 46
- ■ gold
- ☒ white

Stained glass

Charles Rennie Mackintosh was a Scottish craftsman of the Art Nouveau period, and his favourite motif was the rose. The cross-stitch design for this pretty and practical needlecase is based on the stylised roses he used in his stained glass work.

Materials
Piece pink Aida fabric 6 × 12in
    (15 × 30cm), 14 threads to 1in (2.5cm)
Piece of pink cotton (or polyester/cotton)
    fabric 6 × 12in (15 × 30cm)
Piece bright pink felt, 4½ × 8in
    (11.5 × 20cm)
Anchor stranded cottons as follows: one
    skein each of 78 crimson, 63 dark pink,
    52 pink, 50 pale pink, 73 very pale
    pink, 236 dark grey

Preparation
1 Fold and mark the middle of the Aida fabric. On the right-hand side, measure and mark the middle with lines of basting stitches, vertically and horizontally.

Working the design
2 The middle of the chart is indicated by arrows on the edges. This corresponds with the middle of your embroidery area, marked with basting threads.

3 Stitch the design following the chart. Use six strands of embroidery cotton together and work stitches over two threads of the fabric.

Finishing
4 Place the embroidery and pink fabric together, right sides facing. Sew or stitch the two pieces together round 3 sides, turn to right side and press. Turn in edges, oversew together.

5 Fold the piece in half to find the midway line, and do the same with the piece of felt. Stitch the felt to the inside of the needlecase along the fold line.

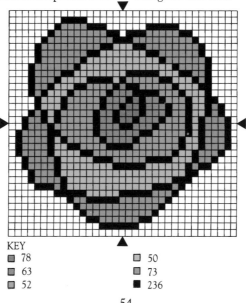

KEY
■	78	▢	50
■	63	▢	73
▢	52	■	236

Easy as ABC

This alphabet can be worked up as a sampler just as it is, or individual letters can be used to personalise all kinds of clothes and accessories from dressing gowns and babies' dresses to bags and belts. On page 58, there's a different way of working them in two colours. Choose shades that complement the item you are personalising.

Alphabet letters

In Victorian households, house linens – bedsheets, pillowcases, towels, tablecloths, traycloths and napkins – were often marked with cross-stitched initials, rather than spoiling the linens with marking ink. Initials were also worked on many personal items such as handkerchiefs, purses, scarves and shawls, underclothes and nightgowns, as well as on children's and babies' garments. Sometimes tiny flowers and leaves were incorporated to make the initials even prettier.

The alphabet charts on pages 57 and 58 can be worked to any scale you like. On fabric with 14 threads to 1in (2.5cm), the letters would be just over 1in (2.5cm) high.

Worked on a finer weave fabric, the resulting letters will be smaller.

Alphabet letters are an ideal way of decorating and personalising embroidered items. You can use just one letter, perhaps surrounding it with a garland of flowers, or use two or three letters for the initials of a name. Worked in two colours and with some parts outlined in back stitch, letters from either of the charts can be overlapped. Try working a man's initials on the pocket of a dressing gown – remove the pocket first and use the waste canvas method described on page 34. You can work your own initials on lingerie cases, or handkerchief sachets, or make a prettily embroidered pillow, complete with initials for a bridal gift.

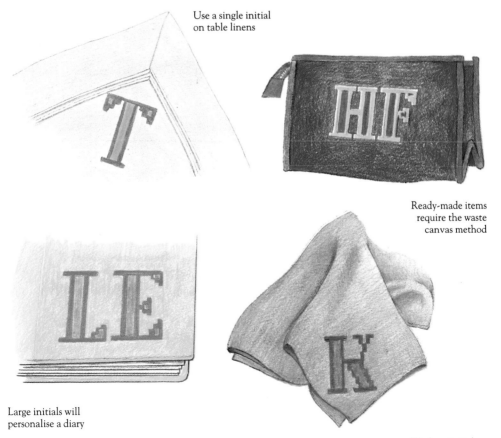

Use a single initial on table linens

Ready-made items require the waste canvas method

Large initials will personalise a diary

Work an initial on a scarf for a gift

Under glass

Chinese brocades were the inspiration for this beautiful pattern, made even more exotic by the use of bright shiny threads. A backing of imitation gold kid adds to the richness.

Materials
3½in (9cm) diameter glass paperweight blank
White Hardanger fabric, 4in (10cm) square, 11 threads to 1in (2.5cm)
Marlitt viscose thread as follows: one skein each of 863 pink, 837 blue, 819 purple
Light-weight iron-on interfacing, 4in (10cm) square
Gold metallic thread
Circle of imitation gold leather, 3½in (9cm) diameter; clear glue.

Preparation
1 Measure and mark the middle of the fabric with lines of basting stitches, vertically and horizontally.

Working the embroidery
2 The middle of the chart is indicated by arrows on the edges. This corresponds with the middle of your fabric, marked with basting.

3 Using all four strands of the viscose thread, then four strands of gold thread together, work the design following the chart and key.

Finishing
4 Iron the interfacing on to the back of the embroidery to prevent fraying. Make sure the iron is not too hot or the metallic threads could melt.

5 Trim carefully round the circle of embroidery, close to the stitching, but taking care not to cut the stitches.

6 Slip the embroidery into the indentation at the bottom of the paperweight, right side up, so that it shows through the glass top. Spread clear glue across the top of the gold circle and press into position on the bottom of the paperweight, so that the gold shows through the glass. Leave to dry.

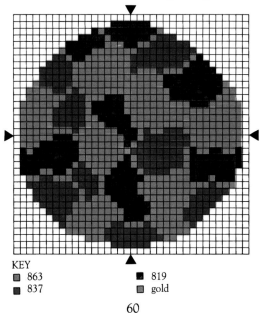

KEY
■ 863
■ 837
■ 819
▨ gold

Shy violets

Here's a pretty flower motif that can be worked on a pocket of a skirt or blouse. It is a motif you'll use again and again, for clothes, accessories or even for home furnishings.

Materials
Anchor stranded cottons as follows: one skein each of 101 dark purple, 112 mid-purple, 98 mauve, 342 pale mauve, 218 dark green, 216 pale green, 302 yellow

Note: If you are making your own garment, embroider the pocket before you attach it. On a ready-made garment, remove the pocket, and then stitch it back into place once it is embroidered. If you are using an evenweave fabric, such as linen or a linen-look weave, you will be able to embroider the motif directly onto the fabric working the cross stitches over an even number of threads – three or four, depending on the thickness of the weave. If the fabric is satin,

cotton twill or a similar type, use the waste canvas method (see page 36).

Preparation
1 Measure and mark the middle of the pocket with lines of basting stitches, vertically and horizontally.

Working the embroidery
2 The arrows on the chart edges indicate the middle of the design. This corresponds with the marked middle of your fabric. Embroider the design, starting in the middle, following the chart and key.

Finishing
3 When the embroidery is completed, press lightly on the wrong side to 'emboss' the design. Sew the pocket to the garment.

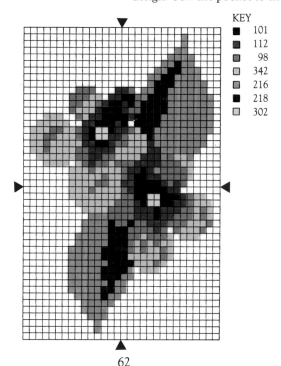

KEY
■ 101
■ 112
▨ 98
□ 342
▨ 216
■ 218
□ 302

Luxurious lingerie

Add a touch of luxury to lingerie, with a columbine embroidered in real silk onto a satin negligée. The traditional English wayside flower has been turned into a delicate motif, and using the waste canvas method means that you can work the embroidery onto the most delicate fabrics.

Materials

Piece of waste canvas, 4in (10cm) square, 12 threads to 1in (2.5cm)

Madeira embroidery silks as follows: one skein each of 613 pale pink, 701 mid-pink, 703 dark pink, 1309 pale green, 1311 mid-green, 1312 dark green.

Preparation

1 Baste the waste canvas onto the shoulder of the negligée over the place where the motif is to be. Measure and mark the middle of the canvas with basting stitches both vertically and horizontally.

Working the embroidery

2 Using all four strands of the silk together, stitch the design following the chart and key, and starting in the middle indicated by arrows on the edges of the chart.

Finishing

3 Remove the waste canvas by dampening it to dissolve the glue holding the threads together. Pull each strand of canvas from under the embroidery, leaving the cross-stitch design on the surface of the fabric. This technique is described and illustrated on page 37.

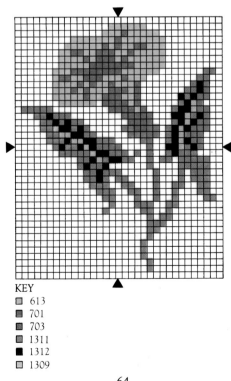

KEY
☐ 613
▨ 701
▨ 703
▨ 1311
■ 1312
☐ 1309

Oriental splendour

The shape of an oriental fan is used for this pretty clutch purse. It is worked in wool embroidery on hessian for everyday use, but the design would look magnificent stitched in metallic threads on a glittery fabric for a luxurious evening bag.

A

The instructions for working this design, and making up the bag, are on pages 68–69

KEY

654	▨
85	◼
3000	▣
311	▢

Materials
Circle of blue hessian, 19in (48cm)
    diameter, approximately 16 threads to
    1in (2.5cm)
Circle of pelmet-weight iron-on interfacing
    the same size
Circle of blue lining fabric the same size
Anchor tapisserie wools as follows: one skein
    each of 311 pale yellow, 3000 dark
    yellow, 85 pink, 654 green.

Preparation
1 Divide the fabric circle into quarters with
basting stitches.

Working the embroidery
2 Work the design in one quarter, following
the chart and key, making sure that point A
on the design is towards the centre of the
circle. Work each cross stitch across two
threads of the hessian.

Finishing
3 Press the finished embroidery on the
wrong side with a warm iron. Check that the
fabric is square. Press again and pull into
shape if it has distorted. Iron the interfacing
circle to the wrong side of the embroidery.

4 Cut out one quarter of the embroidered
fabric (see illustration) leaving a ½in (12mm)
seam allowance.

5 Cut out one quarter of the lining fabric.
With right sides together, pin and baste the
embroidered fabric to the lining, leaving the
edge marked B open.

6 Machine-stitch ½in (12mm) from the edge
along all the edges except edge B (see
illustration). Clip the corner and into the
seam allowance, then turn right side out.
Press seams flat with a warm iron.

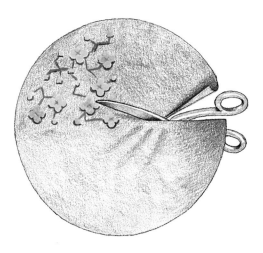

1 Cut out one quarter of hessian, leaving a seam allowance.

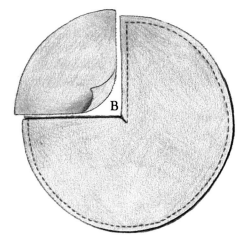

2 Cut out one quarter of the lining, and stitch lining to hessian.

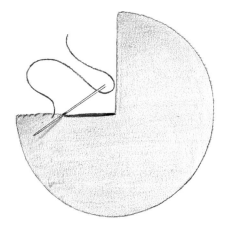

3 Turn right side out, and stitch edge B.

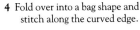

4 Fold over into a bag shape and stitch along the curved edge.

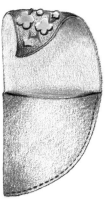

7 Fold in the seam allowances of edge B, and sew together by hand or machine-stitch.

8 Fold the bag (see illustration) and stitch together around the curved edge. Topstitch around the other edges of the bag.

9 Fasten the purse with a press fastener, or work a loop on the flap with matching stranded threads and sew a pretty button on the purse to correspond.

This design is such an unusual shape that it would work well in different sizes. Scale the design down and embroider it on Hardanger or other evenweave fabric for a pincushion, or scale it up and embroider a quarter-circle cushion.

Midnight blues

This amusing cat design shows just how versatile cross-stitch designs can be. Here it is used for a card and on page 73 it becomes a picture.

Materials (for card)
Piece of cream Hardanger fabric, 4 × 5½in (100 × 14cm), 11 threads to 1in (2.5cm)
Piece of blue card, 13½ × 7in (34 × 17.5cm)
Clear glue (or rubber solution)
Anchor stranded cottons as follows: one skein each of 403 black, 46 red, 297 yellow, 132 dark blue, 129 mid-blue, 128 light blue, 244 green, 372 light brown, 374 mid-brown, 381 dark brown, 01 white
Blue rectangular-window card blank.

Preparation
1 Measure and mark the middle of the fabric with lines of basting stitches, vertically and horizontally.

Working the embroidery
2 The middle of the chart is indicated by arrows on the edges. This corresponds with the middle of your fabric, marked with basting.

3 Using three strands of thread together, work the design following the chart and key.

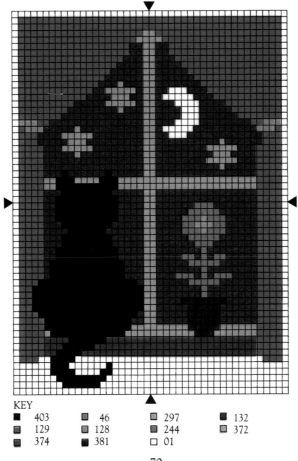

KEY

■ 403	■ 46	■ 297	■ 132
■ 129	■ 128	■ 244	■ 372
■ 374	■ 381	□ 01	

The cat-in-the-window picture here is worked from the same chart as the Midnight blues card on page 71.

4 Fold the blue card into three, and cut a window in the central panel big enough for the embroidery to show through.

Finishing
5 Press the design lightly on the wrong side with a warm iron. Spread glue thinly around the margins of the embroidery.

6 Glue the embroidery behind the window in the central panel.

7 Glue the back of the left-hand panel and fold it over behind the embroidery.

CAT-IN-THE-WINDOW

Materials
Piece of cream Binca fabric, 12 × 14
    (30 × 35cm), 6 threads to 1in (2.5cm)
Anchor soft cottons as follows: one skein
    each of 46 red, 297 yellow, 128 light
    blue, 244 green, 372 light brown,
    374 mid-brown, 381 dark brown,
    01 white; two skeins of 403 black;
    three skeins of 132 dark blue; four
    skeins of 129 mid blue
Piece of Pres-On adhesive board
Masking tape.

Preparation
1 Prepare the fabric as for the card.

Working the embroidery
2 Stitch the design, following the chart and key for Midnight blues on page 70.

3 Press the embroidery on the wrong side with a warm iron.

4 Peel the protective covering from the Pres-On board, and position the embroidery carefully on the top. Smooth the embroidery in place, outwards from the centre.

5 Fold the fabric over the edges of the board and secure at the back with masking tape. The embroidery is now ready for framing.

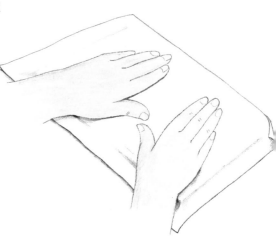

Smooth the fabric on the adhesive surface.

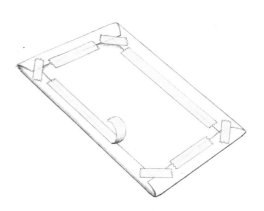

Secure the fabric on the back of the board with masking tape.

Happy ever after

An embroidered frame for a favourite wedding photograph makes an ideal wedding present and it's a lovely idea for a special anniversary gift too. Work it in the pastel colour scheme given or match the colours to the bride's bouquet. The chart is on pages 76–77.

Materials

Piece of white Hardanger, 16 × 20in (40 × 51cm), 22 threads to 1in (2.5cm)
Anchor stranded cottons as follows: one skein each of 120 pale blue, 140 mid-blue, 50 pale pink, 52 mid-pink
Silver metallic thread
Piece of Pres-On adhesive board, 11 × 12½in (28 × 32cm)
Masking tape.

Preparation

1 Measure and mark the middle of the fabric with lines of basting stitches, vertically and horizontally.

Working the embroidery

2 The middle of the chart is indicated by arrows on the edges. (See pages 76–77.) This corresponds with the middle of your fabric marked with basting.

3 Using three strands of thread together, or three strands of metallic thread together, work the design following the chart and key. Work stitches over two threads of fabric.

4 Press the completed embroidery on the wrong side with a cool iron. (A too-hot iron may melt the metallic threads.)

5 Choose a suitable photograph to fit the frame and mark the position on the back of the fabric. Cut a hole from the middle, allowing 1½in (37mm) of fabric for turning.

6 Lay the fabric over the Pres-On board, and carefully mark the position where the photograph will go, using a pin. Cut out the centre of the board with a crafts knife.

7 Peel off the protective backing and press the embroidery firmly onto the adhesive surface. Turn the fabric edges over to the back and secure with masking tape. Clip the corners of the inner edges so that they fold over neatly.

8 Mount the photograph in the centre of the frame, and secure at the back with masking tape.

The hearts and ribbons would look pretty worked on a cushion

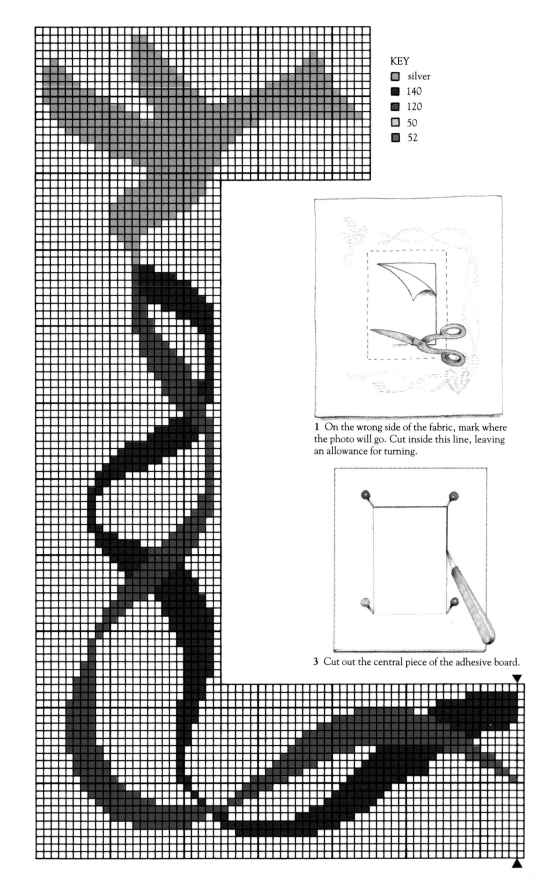

KEY
- □ silver
- ■ 140
- ■ 120
- □ 50
- ■ 52

1 On the wrong side of the fabric, mark where the photo will go. Cut inside this line, leaving an allowance for turning.

3 Cut out the central piece of the adhesive board.

Chart for the Happy ever after frame

The two sections of the chart join
where indicated with arrows

2 Position the fabric over the Pres-On board,
use pins to mark the photo position.

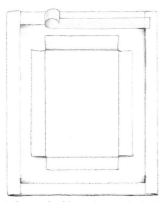

4 Secure the fabric edges on the back
with masking tape.

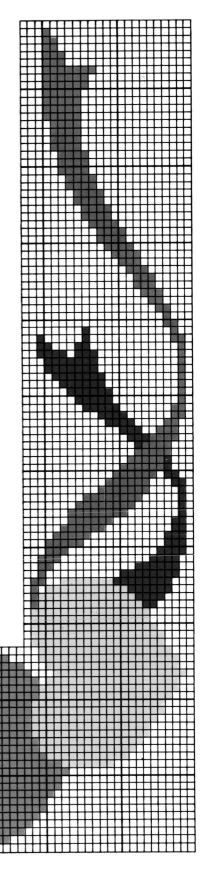

Glittering beauty

Pretty trinkets deserve a special place to keep them; what could be nicer than a glittery dragonfly jewellery box? Plastic canvas is used to construct the box.

Materials

Plastic canvas as follows:
Four pieces 11 × 31 holes (box sides)
Four pieces 5 × 33 holes (lid sides)
Piece 33 × 33 holes (lid top)
Piece 31 × 31 holes (box bottom)
Anchor soft cottons as follows: two skeins of
 01 white, 1 skein of 110 mauve
Twilley's Goldfingering as follows: one spool
 each of WG11 light blue, WG8 dark
 blue.

Working the embroidery

1 The middle of the chart is indicated by arrows on the edges. This corresponds with the middle of your canvas for the lid top.

2 Following the chart and key, embroider the dragonfly design and background on the lid top. Use two strands of Goldfingering together when embroidering the dragonfly.

3 Embroider the lid sides and box sides following the colours shown on the charts.

4 Work the box bottom entirely in white or choose one of the other colours if you prefer.

Constructing the box

5 Make the lid by stitching the pieces of plastic canvas together with cross stitch, using two strands of the pale blue Goldfingering.

6 Make the box bottom the same way, using the dark blue Goldfingering.

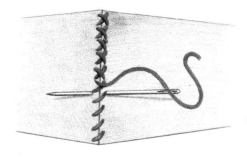

Join pieces of canvas
with cross stitches

Lid
sides

Box
sides

KEY
▨ WG11
▦ 110
■ WG8
▣ 01

78

Baubles, bangles and beads

Cross stitch can also be used to make jewellery using metal embroidery blanks. Stitch yourself a rainbow bracelet and add some gold beads to the embroidery to make a pair of evening earrings.

Bracelet
Materials
Gold N' Cross Stitch bracelet blank in silver finish
Anchor stranded cottons as follows: one skein each of 146 blue, 110 mauve, 41 pink, 323 orange, 302 yellow, 208 green.

Working the embroidery
Using three strands of thread together, work the design following the chart and key.

Earrings
Materials
Pair Gold N' Cross Stitch earring blanks in gold finish
Anchor stranded cotton as follows: one skein of 111 purple
84 tiny gold beads.

Working the embroidery
1 Stitch the plain outside squares of the design first on each earring.

2 For the inner squares, work the first half of the cross stitch, then thread a gold bead onto the needle before completing the top half of the stitch. You may find that you have to change to a finer needle so that it will go through the centre hole of the beads.

Make a pair of earrings to match your most exotic evening gown; choose either gold or silver backgrounds, and beads in the same colour, then pick a shade of stranded cotton which complements the dress. Or, omit the beads and work the central stitches in a glittery metallic thread to catch the light. For a different mood, work a bracelet to match your favourite summer dress. Instead of the rainbow colours shown here, pick the colours from a floral print or striped dress, and use stranded cottons in those shades to produce a unique piece of jewellery.

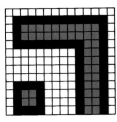

KEY
▨ Gold beads
■ Purple

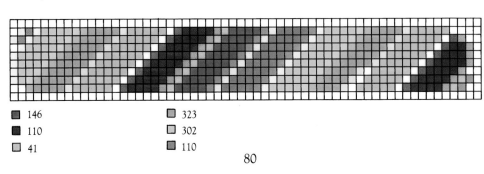

■ 146   ▨ 323
■ 110   □ 302
□ 41   ▨ 110

80

Plains Indian belt

Indian beadwork designs are echoed in this bold zigzag belt; team it with co-ordinating colours, or wear it with white for fashion impact.

Materials
Strip of single-thread canvas 12 threads to
  1in (2.5cm), 2in (5cm) wide, and to
  the waist measurement plus 3in (8cm)
Anchor soft cottons as follows: two skeins
  each of 433 turquoise, 227 green, 28
  pink; three skeins of 133 blue
Strip of medium-weight iron-on interfacing
  1in (2.5cm) wide by the belt length
Metal buckle to fit a 1in (2.5cm) belt

Working the embroidery
1 Begin at the diagonal end of the chart,
12mm (^{1}/2in) from the canvas bottom edge,
and the same distance from the right-hand
end. Work repeats of the design to the other
end of the canvas.

2 Press the unworked canvas edges to the
wrong side with a warm iron. Trim one end
of the iron-on interfacing to the shape of the
diagonal end. Iron the interfacing strip onto
the back of the belt.

3 Turn the square end of the belt over the
bar of the buckle and sew into place.

4 Try the belt on, and make a hole for the
buckle tongue at the appropriate place. (The
tongue will slip in between the stitches.)

Using this method, it's easy to make a
belt to match any of your favourite
outfits. Simply pick out the colours you
want to use to match or complement a
skirt, dress, summer blouse or pair of
trousers, and work the belt in those
shades. You could use a coloured
buckle, too. Or, if you want something
extra-special, work a belt in metallic
threads to add the finishing touch to a
glamorous evening outfit.

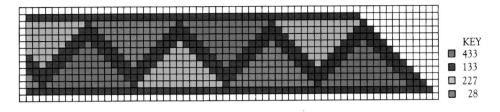

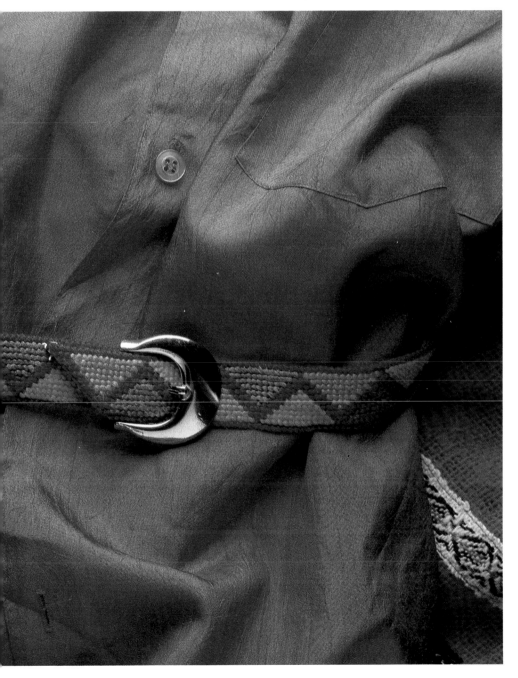

4: SPECIAL OCCASIONS